Debt Structure, Market Value of Firm, and Recovery Rate

Min Qi
Xinlei Zhao

Office of the Comptroller of the Currency

Economics Working Paper 2011-2
October 2011

Keywords: Recovery rate; loss given default (LGD); seniority index; credit risk; debt structure. JEL classifications: G32, G33, G38.

Min Qi is the Deputy Director of the Credit Risk Analysis Division of the Office of the Comptroller of the Currency. Xinlei Zhao is a Financial Economist in the Credit Risk Analysis Division at the Office of the Comptroller of the Currency and an Associate Professor in the Department of Finance, Kent State University. Please address correspondence to Xinlei Zhao, Office of the Comptroller of the Currency, 250 E St. SW, Washington, DC 20219 (202-927-9960; xinlei.zhao@occ.treas.gov). The authors wish to thank Ross Dillard for research assistance, Joyce Jones for editorial assistance, and Sibel Sirakaya Alemdar for helpful comments. We also thank seminar participants at the Office of the Comptroller of the Currency, the SIG Validation Subgroup meeting of the Basel Committee on Banking Supervision, and the interagency Risk Quantification Forum for helpful comments.

Debt Structure, Market Value of Firm, and Recovery Rate

Min Qi
Xinlei Zhao

October 2011

Abstract: This paper examines the determinants of creditor recoveries from defaulted debt instruments, an important yet under-studied area in investment and risk management. First, we argue that to properly measure a debt instrument's relative position in a firm's debt structure, debt pari passu to the instrument must be taken into account. We propose a new measure of seniority and find that it is the most important determinant of recovery rates, explaining more recovery variations than the combination of all commonly used instrument-level variables, including seniority class, collateral type, and percentage above. Second, we find that firm-level variables, especially the trailing 12-month stock returns, are more critical than industry- or macroeconomic-level variables, although the latter can also help, for private firms because stock price information is not available for such firms. In contrast with earlier studies, we find that the relative contribution of the industry and macroeconomic variables varies with the sample, model specification, and especially the modeling technique used.

I. Introduction

Although there are numerous studies on default prediction models, studies on recovery rate, or one minus loss given default (LGD), are very limited. Despite the importance of recovery rate in many aspects of investment and risk management, such as loss forecasting, loan pricing, portfolio valuation, and capital planning, most academic studies and industry models use either constant or random recovery rates. This study intends to advance understanding of recovery rates by addressing two central questions: What are the most important determinants of recovery rates? What are the relative contributions of variables at the instrument, firm, industry, and economy level?

We argue that the existing measures of relative debt seniority, such as the percentage of debt above, cannot fully capture firms' debt structure, because firms have the tendency to issue disproportionately more of one class of debt than other classes (Bris, Ravid, and Sverdlove [2009]; and Colla, Ippolito, and Li [2011]).[1] We therefore propose a new variable, called seniority index, to incorporate the percentage of debt both more senior than and pari passu (that is, at the same rank) to the instrument under consideration. This variable has not been previously investigated in academic literature or industry practice. We find that it is very important to account for debt pari passu, as this new seniority index turns out to be the most crucial determinant of recovery rates. Its explanatory power tops the combined explanatory power from all commonly used instrument-level variables that are covered in this study, including seniority class, collateral type, and percentage above.

We find that after seniority index, firm conditions, measured by trailing stock returns, is the second most important determinant of recovery risks. For private firms, where such stock

---

[1] Further discussion on debt structure and recovery rate is provided in section II.

return information is not available, industry- and macro-level variables can help. Unlike Acharya, Bharath, and Srinivasan (2007), however, we find that the relative contribution of the industry and macroeconomic variables varies with the sample, model specification, and, most importantly, the modeling technique used.

Our findings have several important implications. First, the seniority index variable we propose is different from the percentage above variable used in Moody's LossCalc to measure the percentage of debt that is more senior than the instrument under consideration. Our results show that seniority index is a better measure of an instrument's seniority than the existing seniority measures, such as seniority class indicators, percentage above, or debt cushion (that is, percentage below). Our findings suggest a way to substantially improve the accuracy of pricing and ratings of debt instruments.

Second, the common practice of assuming a constant recovery rate for instruments of the same seniority class might not be appropriate, as the seniority index of the same seniority class could vary widely, due to different debt issuance behavior across firms. Many studies assume a constant recovery rate for each credit rating group.[2] This may not be appropriate, either, as the seniority index has not been used by the rating agencies to date and it could vary significantly within each credit rating group.

Third, because collecting recovery data (including LGD risk factors) are one of the most daunting challenges faced by almost all financial institutions undergoing Basel II implementation, resources should be devoted to collecting data that allow the calculation and

---

[2] Studies that evaluate default predictions from credit models usually use a single default recovery rate for a group of relatively homogeneous bonds. For example, Elton, Gruber, Agrawal, and Mann (2001) use the average recovery rate for each rating group. Huang and Huang (2002) use the recovery rates from Moody's and assume the rates to be the same for bonds of the same seniority and credit rating. Eom, Helwege, and Huang (2004) restrict their sample to firms with fewer than five types of debt, the majority of which is of investment grade. They use 51.31 percent as the recovery rate and conduct robustness testing using 100 percent for the recovery rate. Longstaff, Mithal, and Neis (2005) use a constant recovery rate of 50 percent.

tracking of seniority index, the most important determining factor of LGD. Data vendors should consider doing the same.

Finally, our findings also shed light on the debate over the joint modeling of probability of default (PD) and recovery rate.[3] In the original Merton model (1974), PD and recovery rate are inversely associated, but later extensions of the structural models usually assume recovery rates to be exogenous and independent of PD. Reduced-form models mostly assume recovery rates independent of PD, and the same assumption is made in some vendor credit portfolio value-at-risk models.[4] Recent empirical studies find a negative relationship between default and recovery rates. It is not clear, however, what is driving the relationship—a single systematic risk factor, industry conditions, or firms' idiosyncratic risk.[5] Our finding that recovery rates are driven more by firm-level variables than by industry- or macro-level variables suggests that recovery rates have a large idiosyncratic component. Earlier studies, such as Duffie, Eckner, Horel, and Saita (2009), Tang and Yan (2010), and Qi, Zhang, and Zhao (2009), find that defaults are mainly driven by firm-level risk factors. Together, these findings suggest that the joint distribution of default and recovery is more likely due to idiosyncratic risk than to systematic risk.

In the next section, we discuss and develop a more proper measure of debt seniority. In section III, we describe the sample. Section IV reports the empirical results, and section V summarizes several robustness checks that we performed. The final section states our conclusions.

---

[3] See, for example, Acharya, Bharath, and Srinivasan (2007); Altman, Brady, Resti, and Sironi (2005); Altman, Resti, and Sironi (2001); Frye (2000a, 2000b, and 2000c); Pykhtin (2003); and de Servigny and Renault (2004).

[4] For example, J.P. Morgan's CreditMetrics (Gupton, Finger, and Bhatia, 1997) and Credit Suisse Financial Products' CreditRisk+.

[5] See Altman, Resti, and Sironi (2005) for detailed discussions.

II. Measure of Debt Seniority

The most common measure of debt seniority in literature and in banking practice is instrument type (or seniority class, such as bank loans, senior secured bonds, senior unsecured bonds, senior subordinated bonds, subordinated bonds, and junior bonds).[6] We argue that these simple indicators do not show relative position of a debt instrument in a firm's debt structure. Rauh and Sufi (2010) find that different types of firms tend to have different debt structure— firms with high credit quality mainly rely on senior unsecured debt, whereas firms with lower credit quality usually use multiple tiers of debt, including bank loans, secured, senior unsecured, and subordinated debts. As a result, unsecured debts from different firms may not be directly comparable, and recovery from unsecured debts may not necessarily be lower than secured debts.[7]

More importantly, we argue that some of the more sophisticated measures of relative seniority that have been used up to now, such as percentage of debt above or debt cushion below, cannot always properly capture a debt instrument's position in a firm's debt structure, either. This is because both Bris, Ravid, and Sverdlove (2009) and Colla, Ippolito, and Li (2011) find that firms show a tendency to issue disproportionately more of one particular type of debt than other types, rendering the percentage of debt above (debt cushion) less informative of the firm's debt structure, especially for the most senior (junior) class of debt instrument. This point can be illustrated via two simple examples. In the first example, firm A and firm B, are in similar financial conditions and have outstanding senior secured and junior bonds, but firm A has more senior secured bonds, while firm B has more junior bonds. In this example, the proportion of

---

[6] See, for example, Altman and Kishore (1996); Gupton, Gates, and Carty (2000); de Servigny and Renault (2004); and Varma and Cantor (2005).

[7] This is confirmed by the internal analysis of several large U.S. banks that shows cases in which higher recovery is observed from unsecured debts than from secured debts.

senior secured bonds is 80 percent for firm A and 20 percent for firm B. Even though the senior secured bonds of both firms have zero percent above, the recovery rate of the senior secured bonds is likely to be higher for firm B than for firm A. A similar argument can be made for the junior debt. The recovery rate of the junior bonds is expected to be higher for firm B than for firm A, even though the junior bonds of both firms have zero debt cushion.

In the second example, consider a firm that is valued at $22 million in assets with $20 million of debt. Upon default, the asset value will drop to $14 million. The firm has two types of debt outstanding: $10 million in senior secured bonds and $10 million in senior unsecured bonds. If the firm defaults, the recovery rate will be 100 percent for the senior secured bonds and 40 percent for the senior unsecured bonds. Suppose the senior unsecured bonds mature and the firm replaces them with a new issue, with 60 percent in senior secured bonds and 40 percent in senior unsecured bonds.[8] With this change in debt structure, the percentage of the firm's senior secured bonds increases from 50 percent to 80 percent, and consequently, the recovery rate of the firm's senior secured bonds drops from 100 percent to 87.5 percent, even though the senior secured bonds still have no debt above it. Recovery from the senior unsecured bonds also change from 40 percent to zero as a result of the new issue, even though its debt cushion remains zero before and after the new issue.

Both examples clearly show that percentage above or debt cushion cannot always properly measure debt seniority. An appropriate measure of relative seniority should account for not only the percentage of debt above or below but also the percentage of debt pari passu. As such, we create a new instrument-level variable "seniority index," which is defined as one minus percentage above minus one-half percentage pari passu. Because the choice of one-half of

---

[8] In practice, it is not uncommon for banks to convert unsecured loans into secured or partially secured loans when firms' financial conditions deteriorate.

percentage pari passu in the definition of seniority index is rather arbitrary, we also define two alternatives, incorporating one-third and two-thirds of percentage pari passu, respectively.

Everything else being equal, the lower the percentage pari passu, the higher the relative seniority of a debt instrument in a firm's debt structure, the larger share of the pie the creditor of that debt instrument can claim in the event of default, and the higher the recovery should be. How much additional explanatory power is added by factoring in percentage pari passu, however, is an empirical question, which we will address in sections III and IV.

The most common LGD drivers in practice are collateral types. It is very likely, however, that a proper measure of relative seniority can outweigh collateral types in recovery rate models. The conventional wisdom that recovery varies across collateral types assumes that upon default, creditors take possession of collaterals and sell them. Because collaterals such as inventory and accounts receivable are easier to liquidate, defaulted debts with these collaterals are believed to have higher recoveries. Default resolutions, however, often do not involve collateral sale. The most frequent resolution type in our sample is Chapter 11 reorganization, in which creditors cannot take possession of collaterals due to the automatic stay provision, except when the debt is secured by aircraft equipment and vessels, or when the case is dismissed or converted to liquidation under Chapter 7 if the reorganization plan cannot be confirmed.

Other resolution approaches commonly used by banks are out-of-court settlement and sale of defaulted instruments in the market for distressed debts, which do not involve collateral sale either. Although collateral types might affect the outcome of these resolution types, many other factors such as banks' workout strategy and expertise, difficulty of reaching agreement among various creditors, price and liquidity in the distressed debt market, etc., can be influential as well. Therefore, there may not be a strong link between collateral types and recovery in these resolution types.

Even in the case of collateral sale, the impact of collateral types may not be prominent for two reasons. First, firms in financial distress might devote few resources to resolving customer complaints, maintaining equipment, and safeguarding fixed investments, resulting in uncertainty in values of collaterals, such as accounts receivable, autos, and real estate. Second, even though some collateral types, such as accounts receivable and cash, may be relatively safe, recovery rate of defaulted debts secured by these collateral types can still be low if collateral coverage is low (that is, loan-to-value ratio is high). Because of the usual lack of accurately updated collateral coverage information,[9] it is hard to determine whether and to what extent differences in recoveries across collateral types are due to differences in collateral coverage. Lastly, a debt instrument can be secured by multiple collateral types. It may not be practical to accurately estimate a separate recovery rate for each collateral type.

III. Sample

Our sample is from Moody's Ultimate Recovery Database (URD). The data cover U.S. corporate default events with more than $50 million in debt at the time of default. Three approaches to calculating recovery rates, namely, the settlement method, the trading price method, and the liquidity event method, show the outcomes of three different workout strategies.[10] The database also shows the preferred method, which reflects the best valuation of a given default based on the knowledge and experience of Moody's analysts. We thus use the

---

[9] Ideally, collateral coverage ratio should be considered and updated as needed. This variable is rarely available or used by banks, however, due to the cost and the lack of accurate methods of updating some of the collateral values.

[10] The settlement method uses the earliest available trading prices of the instruments received in a settlement. The trading price method uses the trading prices of pre-petition instruments at the time of emergence. The liquidity event method uses the value of illiquid assets, such as subsequent acquisitions, at liquidation.

recovery rates from the preferred method. To obtain discounted ultimate recoveries, URD discounts each nominal recovery back to the last time when interest was paid using the instrument's pre-petition coupon rate. We also require firm-level information (in particular, distance-to-default information) available from Compustat and the Center for Research in Security Prices (CRSP). Our sample consists of 1,449 observations from 1987 to 2009.[11] This sample is substantially larger than the 239 observations (including distance-to-default) from 1982 to 1999 used in Acharya, Bharath, and Srinivasan (2007).[12]

Panel A of table 1 shows the sample distribution and recovery rates by year. There are more observations during 2001 and 2002, which coincides with higher default rates in those two years. The lowest recovery rate is observed in 1989, and the highest recovery rate is observed in 1992. During the sample period, the mean recovery rate is 56.33 percent.

Panel B shows the sample breakdown by instrument type and collateral type.[13] Senior unsecured bonds constitute the largest proportion, followed by revolvers, senior secured bonds, and term loans. Junior bonds constitute the smallest share of the sample. The recovery rate declines monotonically from revolvers to junior bonds, consistent with the expectation following the absolute priority rule that more senior and secured instruments do better.

---

[11] The majority of the defaults in our samples are bankruptcy (85.37 percent), followed by distressed exchange (13.53 percent).

[12] The data used in Acharya, Bharath, and Srinivasan (2007) are from Portfolio Management Data (PMD). Moody's bought PMD and expanded the recovery data coverage. Therefore, the Moody's URD data we use in this study are more comprehensive and up to date.

[13] We use the category most assets if the collateral type in URD is most assets (all assets excluding inventory and account receivables), all assets, PP&E (property, plant, and equipment), and all noncurrent assets. We separate out equipment because the recovery of this collateral type is much lower than all the types in most assets. We group oil and gas properties and real estate into other assets because of the low number of observations in these two collateral types and the minimal difference in their recovery rates. We retain the collateral types guarantees and intercompany debt despite their low number of observations, because these types are quite unusual and the recovery rates are different from other types. We classify cash in the same group as inventory and receivables because they are all liquid assets and have similar recovery rates. On the other hand, capital stock, with which cash is often grouped, has a much lower recovery rate in this sample.

Slightly more than half of the debt instruments in our sample are unsecured, and the recovery rates from these instruments are quite low. Guarantee means that a separately rated entity guaranteed the company (e.g., Motorola for Iridium). This collateral type is rare for large public companies, and it provides the highest recovery rate. Inventory, receivables, and cash also provide good collateral values with high recovery rates. Capital stock has a lower recovery rate than inventory, receivables, and cash. This is not surprising, because a large proportion of this type of collateral is the company's own stock, which is not worth much at time of default. Recoveries from most assets and other assets are also quite high. Recovery rates from equipment are quite low. A possible explanation for this is that equipment is industry- or firm-specific, and thus may not command a high value in a fire sale. The recovery rates of second liens and third liens are comparable to or higher than those of unsecured. These numbers suggest that second- and third-lien holders may not be in the worst shape at time of default.

We also observe a wide variation in recovery rates within each instrument and collateral type.[14] In almost every instrument or collateral type, the minimum recovery rate is 0 percent, the maximum recovery rate is 100 percent, and the recovery rates show a bimodal distribution, indicating that creditors often lose almost nothing or almost everything at default.

Table 2 provides summary statistics of the explanatory variables used in this study.[15] Distance-to-default is a measure of volatility-adjusted leverage and is backed out of the Merton (1974) model;[16] the mean (median) market distance-to-default is 16.75 (15.67). We use all firms covered in Moody's Default Risk Service Database (DRS) to calculate the aggregate and

---

[14] We do not report these statistics because of space limitations. They are available upon request.

[15] We winsorize 1 percent of the observations at both tails to reduce the effect of possibly spurious outliers.

[16] Monthly volatility is estimated as the volatility of daily returns during the month. We use Compustat quarterly leverage data. We would like to thank Shumway for providing the SAS codes.

industry default rates and to compute other aggregate or industry-level variables using the entire CRSP/Compustat data. The NYSE-NASDAQ-AMEX value-weighted index is used as the market return, and its mean is very low at 0.03 percent. This can be explained by the fact that many of our observations are from the 2001–2002 recession.

We use the Fama-French 12-industry group definition. The mean (median) industry distance-to-default is 14.81 (12.77). These numbers are lower than those of the aggregate distance-to-default. Further, the trailing 12-month default rate is higher at the industry level than at the aggregate level. Neither finding is surprising because defaulted firms are likely from distressed industries. In addition, firms in this sample appear to be from industries with little or no profitability—mean and median industry return on assets (ROA) are both negative.[17] Further, firm-level characteristics indicate that these firms are the worst performers in the troubled industries: Compared to those at the industry level, the firm ROA is even lower, firm distances-to-default is much smaller, and firm leverage is much higher.[18]

The variable percentage above measures the percentage of obligations that are more senior than the debt instrument in the debt structure of each defaulted firm. So the larger this variable is, the more junior (or less senior) the instrument is. This variable is included among the explanatory variables in Moody's LossCalc. Seniority index is the new instrument-level variable as discussed in section II to properly measure debt seniority, and seniority indices 2 and 3 incorporate one-third and two-thirds instead of one-half of percentage pari passu as in seniority

---

[17] ROA is defined as the ratio of income before extraordinary items (Compustat data item 18) to total assets (Compustat data item 6).

[18] Leverage is defined as the ratio of long-term debt (Compustat data item 9) plus debt in current liabilities (Compustat data item 34) to total assets (Compustat data item 6). Tangibility is defined as the ratio of property, plant, and equipment (Compustat data item 8) to total assets (Compustat data item 6).

index. Not surprisingly, seniority index 2 has a higher mean than seniority index, whereas seniority index 3 has a lower mean than seniority index.

Panel B of table 2 shows the correlations between these variables and the recovery rate. The recovery rate has the lowest correlation in absolute values with the variable percentage above and the highest correlation with seniority index. These results provide the first piece of evidence that it is important to account for debt pari passu when investigating recovery risk. Due to space limitations, we report only results using the seniority index throughout the rest of the paper. Results using seniority indices 2 and 3 are not materially different.

IV. Empirical Results

To establish robustness, we report the results from two modeling methods: nonparametric regression tree and parametric fractional response regression.[19] The most appealing feature of the regression tree for our study is its ability to handle many explanatory variables (some are highly correlated) at the same time and to split by the most important explanatory variables before splitting by the less important ones. Although over-fitting can be a serious problem, Qi and Zhao (2011) found that the regression tree method's predictive performance on recovery rates is quite stable when cross-validation is used to control for model complexity. Fractional response regression was proposed by Papke and Wooldridge (1996) to model a continuous variable ranging between 0 and 1. Qi and Zhao (2011) found that this method produces a better model fit than other parametric methods, including ordinary least squares (OLS) for LGD modeling.

---

[19] See Qi and Zhao (2011) for more detailed description and comparison of these and other modeling methods of recovery rates. We do not report OLS results in this paper as Qi and Zhao (2011) found that regression tree and fractional response regression provide a better fit than OLS when modeling recovery. As will be discussed in section V, this conclusion also holds in this sample. Furthermore, statistical inferences based on OLS are largely consistent with those from the fractional response regression reported here. The OLS results are available upon request.

Results From the Regression Tree

We include in the regression tree all instrument-level variables indicating instrument type and collateral type, as well as seniority index and percentage above. We also include five firm-level variables (ROA, leverage, tangibility, distance-to-default, and trailing 12-month stock return), six industry-level variables (industry distance-to-default, trailing 12-month industry default rate, industry tangibility, industry leverage, trailing 12-month industry stock return, and industry ROA) and four macro-level variables (trailing 12-month aggregate default rate, trailing 12-month stock market return, aggregate distance-to-default, and the three-month T-bill rate). Following the literature (Acharya, Bharath, and Srinivasan [2007]; Altman and Kishore [1996]), a utility industry dummy variable is also included because the utility industry has a significantly higher recovery rate than other industries in our sample.

Figure 1 presents results from such a regression tree, and we report the in-sample and 5-fold cross-validation R-squared and sum of squared error (SSE) from each step in panel A of table 3. The first split is by seniority index—327 observations that are above the 70.58 percent cutoff value have a mean recovery rate of 90.78 percent, whereas the 1,122 observations with a seniority index below the 70.58 percent cutoff value have an average recovery rate of 46.30 percent, consistent with the expectation that the higher the seniority index of an instrument, the higher the recovery rate. With these two averages as the predicted recovery rates, the split yields an R-squared of 0.231 and an SSE of 166.4 (from panel A of table 3). The second split is along the trailing 12-month stock return. Among the 1,122 observations with seniority index below 70.58 percent, those with a lower stock return have a lower average recovery rate, again as expected. This second step yields an R-squared of 0.385 and an SSE of 133.27.

We require each leaf to have a minimum of 100 observations, so there are only nine splits for the 1,449 observations. After the ninth split, we have an R-squared of 0.540 and an SSE of 99.62. The splits are along six distinctive variables: seniority index, trailing 12-month stock return, percentage above, aggregate distance-to-default, industry leverage, and firm tangibility. Most industry condition variables (such as industry distance-to-default, trailing 12-month industry default rate, industry stock return, and industry ROA) are not picked up by this regression tree. In contrast, the tree does pick up aggregate distance-to-default, which is a measure of macroeconomic conditions. None of the instrument-type or collateral-type variables is picked up by the tree. The utility industry dummy, whose explanatory power is likely absorbed by the six variables included in the tree, also is not picked up by the tree. Further, the five-fold cross-validation results in panel A of table 3 show that the performance of the tree is quite stable.

Figure 2 shows the contribution of each variable in explaining the recovery rate variations. This figure shows that there are two splits each along seniority index, trailing stock returns, and percentage above, and one split each along the other three variables. The total variation in recovery rate explained by this model is 116.93, of which 53.07 (or 45 percent) is by the two splits along the seniority index, 33.35 (or 28.5 percent) is by the two splits along the trailing stock returns, and 21.06 (or 18 percent) is by percentage above. The remaining three splits account for roughly 8.5 percent of the total explained variation. It is thus clear from figure 2 that seniority index is the most important explanatory variable; its explanatory power is more than twice that of percentage above.[20] Firm trailing 12-month stock return is the second most important variable. Combining the impact from stock return and firm tangibility, we conclude

---

[20] We refrain from saying that seniority index is the most important among all potential factors determining the recovery rate, however, as the URD data used in this study do not have information on collateral coverage or loan-to-value ratio (LTV). LTV may carry substantial explanatory power of the recovery rate, especially for secured debt instruments. Such information, however, is often missing in public data as well as banks' internal data. Additional research can be carried out when such data become available.

that the firm-level variables contribute to roughly 30 percent of the explained variations. Industry and macro-level variables contribute to about 6 percent of the total explained variation.[21] Unlike Acharya, Bharath, and Srinivasan (2007), we do not find a strong impact from industry conditions when all variables are included.

Contribution of Seniority Index, Percentage Above, and Other Instrument-Level Variables

To better understand the contribution of the seniority index and percentage above in explaining the recovery risk, we exclude these two variables from the regression tree one at a time. Figure 3 reports the variable contribution when percentage above is excluded from the tree.[22] We find that this tree has 11 splits, leading to an R-squared of 0.568. Therefore, the explanatory power of this tree without percentage above is slightly higher than the tree in figures 1 and 2. Seniority index thus appears to have the ability to absorb the information imbedded in percentage above. With percentage above excluded from the regression tree, more explanatory power is concentrated in seniority index, which accounts for 54 percent of the total explained variation in recovery rates—an increase of 9 percentage points over the corresponding number in figure 2.

By contrast, when we exclude seniority index from the tree, model fits shows a decline: Total variation explained drops from 117 to 113 and the R-squared of the tree declines from 0.54 in table 3 to 0.52 in figure 4. With the absence of seniority index, percentage above picks up some explanatory power; however, a large proportion of the explanatory power shifts to firm-level variables. As a result, the explanatory power of percentage above is outweighed by that of

---

[21] We find that the regression tree built only on instrument-level and firm-level variables on this sample has an R-squared of 0.547 (we do not report these results due to space limitations). This result again shows that, based on this technique, industry and macro variables may have a minor effect on recovery rate.

[22] For the rest of this paper, we report only the variable contributions, but not the trees, due to space limitations.

firm-level variables combined. These results suggest that percentage above misses much of the information content of the seniority index.

In figures 3 and 4, none of the other instrument-level variables, such as instrument type and collateral type, is picked up by the regression tree. To better understand the explanatory power of instrument-level variables, we report in figure 5 variable contributions of a regression tree without seniority index or percentage above. It is clear that when seniority index and percentage above are both excluded, other instrument-level variables, such as revolver, most assets, and unsecured, become important. Therefore, the explanatory power of the instrument type and collateral type variables are likely trumped by seniority index and percentage above in figures 1–4. Furthermore, the explanatory power of the tree in figure 5 is around 20 percent lower than it is in figures 1–4.

Many collateral types, such as inventory, receivables, cash, and equipment, have fewer than 100 observations in the sample (panel B of table 1). Since we require each leaf to have no fewer than 100 observations, one can argue that the finding that the collateral types are not picked up in figures 1–5 might be due to this leaf size floor. To address this concern, variable contributions from different leaf size requirements are reported in panel B of table 3. It is clear from this panel that our earlier conclusion does not change, as long as seniority index and/or percentage above is included in the regression tree. Even when we reduce the minimum size requirement to 20 observations at each leaf, instrument types and collateral types are still not picked up by the trees.[23]

---

[23] This finding does not change even if we reduce the minimum size requirement to five observations at each leaf. These results are not reported here due to space limitations and are available upon request.

Contribution of Firm, Industry, and Macroeconomic Variables

Figures 2–5 all show that the firm's trailing 12-month stock return is the second most important driver of recovery rate after the seniority index, but industry conditions do not play an important role. Our finding on the industry conditions differs from that of Acharya, Bharath, and Srinivasan (2007), who find that industry conditions are still important after controlling for firm-level variables.[24]

Since Acharya, Bharath, and Srinivasan (2007) do not include trailing firm stock returns, seniority index, or percentage above in their analysis, we now exclude these variables.[25] The resulting regression tree is shown in figure 6. This tree yields nine splits along eight variables, with industry distance-to-default being the second most important factor after the instrument type revolver. In contrast, the combined contribution from other firm-level variables (that is, firm distance-to-default, leverage, ROA, and tangibility) is less than half that of industry distance-to-default. The contribution from macro-level variables is also minimal. These results are consistent with Acharya, Bharath, and Srinivasan (2007): Industry variables play a very significant role in default recovery and the impact of the macro variables is marginal. Therefore, their conclusions on industry conditions hold only if the firm's trailing stock returns is not included in the model or for private firms that do not have stock prices.[26] Further, the model fit produced by this tree is substantially lower than that from figure 5, highlighting the importance of the information content embedded in firm stock returns.

---

[24] We do not include median industry Q, the ratio of market value to book value of the firm - a proxy for asset growth prospect, in the regression tree. We find that the relation between recovery rate and industry Q in our sample is different from that documented in Acharya, Bharath, and Srinivasan (2007) probably due to sample difference. Further, inclusion of industry Q does not change our conclusions.

[25] We do not include seniority index and percentage above in figure 6 to make the results more comparable to Acharya, Bharath, and Srinivasan (2007). Including either of these variables or both does not change our conclusion here.

[26] We will later show that such a finding is also sensitive to different modeling techniques.

17

Fractional Response Regression

Table 4 shows results from the fractional response regression. All R-squared reported for fractional response regressions are adjusted R-squared. We show results using instrument types and collateral types in panel A. The base case for instrument types is subordinated bonds, and the base case for collateral types is most assets. Model 1 includes the instrument-type and the utility industry dummy variables. Revolvers, term loans, senior secured bonds, senior unsecured bonds, and senior subordinated bonds all have significantly higher recovery rates than subordinated bonds, and junior bonds have significantly lower recovery rates than subordinated bonds. Further, recovery rates are significantly higher in the utility industry. Combined, these variables explain 26 percent of the recovery rate variations, with an SSE of 160.27.

In model 2, we include the collateral-type and utility industry dummy variables. Compared with the base collateral type of most assets, capital stocks, equipment, unsecured, and third lien have significantly lower recovery rates, while inventory, receivables, and cash have significantly higher recovery rates. The non-significant results on guarantees and inter-company debt are primarily due to small number of observations. There is no significant difference in recovery rates between debt backed by most assets and debt backed by other assets, or second liens at the 5 percent significance level. These results are consistent with the descriptive statistics in table 1. The coefficient for the utility industry dummy is again significantly positive. Combined, these variables explain 22.5 percent of the variation in the recovery risk, with an SSE of 166.71. The model fit is slightly better when instrument types are included.

Model 3 includes all instrument-type and collateral-type variables, as well as the utility dummy. Conclusions on the coefficient estimates in this column do not differ much from models

1 and 2 except that third lien is no longer significant. All combined, these variables explain about 29 percent of the recovery rate variation.

Contribution of Seniority Index, Percentage Above, and Other Instrument-Level Variables

In panel B of table 4, we report the results of six models. Model 4 has only two explanatory variables: the seniority index and the utility industry dummy, both of which have a significant positive association with recovery, as expected. These two variables explain 33 percent of the variation in recovery rates, higher than those of models 1–3.

To compare the explanatory power of the seniority index and percentage above, we include in model 5 percentage above and the utility industry dummy. Percentage above has a significant negative association with recovery, which is intuitive. The adjusted R-squared of model 5, however, is only 23 percent, which is lower than that of model 4, suggesting that percentage above has much lower explanatory power than seniority index. Furthermore, the adjusted R-squared of model 5 is even lower than those of models 1 and 3, indicating that in a fractional response regression LGD model, percentage above does not enjoy much advantage over the use of instrument-type and collateral-type variables. Since it is more difficult to collect and update percentage above than the conventional instrument types and collateral types, this finding may explain the prevalent use of collateral types and sometimes instrument types, but not percentage above, in predicting LGD in the banking practice.

In model 6, we include both seniority index and percentage above. We find that seniority index is still significant with the right sign, while the sign of percentage above flips. This evidence suggests that seniority index dominates percentage above. Since models 4 and 5 are nested models of model 6, we also test the significance of seniority index and percentage above.

We find that percentage above is not significant, while seniority index is. This finding further confirms the importance of seniority index.

In model 7 we add seniority index to model 3, which boosts the adjusted R-squared from 0.288 to 0.365. SSE drops drastically. This is a substantial improvement in goodness-of-fit. The addition of the seniority index also affects the coefficient estimates of some instrument types and collateral types. In particular, the coefficient estimates for senior subordinated bonds and junior bonds are not significant any more, and those of unsecured, second lien, and third lien become positive.

We then replace seniority index with percentage above and run model 8. We find that this model yields an adjusted R-squared of 0.323, which is lower than that of model 4. Therefore, seniority index alone has more explanatory power than the combination of all other variables at the instrument level, which is a quite striking finding.

In model 9, we include all variables at the instrument level. Again, we find that percentage above has the wrong sign, while seniority index is still a strong recovery predictor. This model yields an adjusted R-squared of 0.367, which is only slightly higher than that of model 7, indicating that percentage above contributes almost nothing in recovery prediction beyond those variables already included in model 7.

Contribution of Firm-Level Variables

Panel C of table 4 shows the impact of the firm-level variables. In all models in panels C and D, we include the instrument-type, collateral-type, and the utility industry dummy variables. We do not report the coefficient estimates on these dummy variables to save space.[27] The first model in panel C is model 7 from panel B, which serves as the basis for comparison of all

---

[27] Results on these dummy variables are very similar to model 7 of panel B.

models in panel C. In models 10–13, we add the firm-level variables one at a time. We find that firm distance-to-default, when used alone, is positively related to recovery; this result makes intuitive sense. The coefficient signs of firm ROA, tangibility, and trailing 12-month stock return are all intuitive and statistically significant. Further, it is clear that stock return makes the largest contribution to model fit, as it boosts the R-squared and reduces the SSE the most from model 7. Model 14 shows that when all four firm-level variables are used, the coefficient of firm distance-to-default becomes negative, which is most likely driven by multi-collinearity. Further, we find that firm distance-to-default in model 14 does not add significant explanatory power in comparison to a nested model excluding this variable, as shown in model 15 in panel D. We thus drop firm distance-to-default in panel D.

Contribution of Industry- and Macroeconomic-Level Variables

The roles played by industry-level and macroeconomic-level variables are examined in panel D of table 4, with model 15 as the basis of comparison for models 16–20. A comparison of models 15 and 16 suggests that adding the industry variables improves the model's predictive power, with the R-squared increasing from 0.498 to 0.552. A comparison of models 15 and 17 shows that the macro variables are also effective in enhancing the model fit, boosting the R-squared from 0.498 to 0.557. When all industry-level and macro-level variables are included, the R-squared further increases to 0.582. These results suggest that both of these variables can help improve recovery prediction, and their impact here is much stronger in fractional response regression than in regression tree models. These results imply that the importance of industry-level and macro-level variables may vary with the choice of modeling methodology.

In models 19 and 20, the firm-level variables are excluded. We find that a combination of instrument-level, the utility dummy, and industry-level variables yields an R-squared of 0.454, whereas a combination of instrument-level, utility dummy, and macroeconomic variables leads to an R-squared of 0.448. Both numbers are lower than that of model 15, suggesting that firm-level variables are more important recovery determinants than either industry or macro variables. Further, model 13 has higher adjusted R-squared than models 19 and 20, implying that, among the firm-level variables, firm trailing 12-month stock return alone is more important than industry conditions or macroeconomic variables. In addition, when trailing 12-month firm stock returns is dropped from model 14, the adjusted R-squared drops to 0.427 (which is lower than those for models 19 and 20).[28] This evidence suggests that without firm trailing stock returns, industry- or macro-level variables would outweigh firm-level variables in driving recovery risk. Therefore, firm trailing stock return is a crucial driver of the recovery rate. These findings are consistent with those from the regression tree.

The finding that recovery rates are driven more by firm-level variables than by industry- or macro-level variables suggests that recovery rates have a large idiosyncratic component. Earlier studies, such as Duffie, Eckner, Horel, and Saita (2009); Tang and Yan (2010); and Qi, Zhang, and Zhao (2009), find that defaults are mainly driven by firm-level risk factors. A combination of these findings suggests that the joint distribution of default and recovery is more likely due to idiosyncratic risk than to systematic risk. This finding has important implications for the joint modeling of default and recovery.

In another finding, models including industry and macro variables (models 16–18) have higher adjusted R-squared than those without (models 10–15), suggesting that banks should include industry and macro information in their LGD modeling, especially when a bank's portfolio contains private firms, for which stock return information is not available.

---

[28] This model is not reported due to space limitations.

Further, a comparison of models 16 and 17, as well as a comparison of models 19 and 20, shows that industry and macro variables may be of similar importance in driving recovery rates in the fractional response regression framework. When firm-level variables are included in the models, macro conditions seem to be slightly more important, and vice versa when firm-level variables are excluded. In addition, we compare the nested models 16 and 17 against model 18 and find that both industry and macro variables add significant explanatory power. These results do not support the findings from figures 2–5, implying that the relative contributions of industry and macroeconomic conditions vary with modeling techniques.

V. Robustness Checks

In this section, we report findings from three sets of sensitivity analyses we performed to investigate whether our conclusions are robust. The empirical analyses discussed in this section are not included due to space limitations and are available upon request.

Contribution of Industry and Macro Variables From OLS

Our findings differ from those of Acharya, Bharath, and Srinivasan (2007) in two aspects: (1) industry conditions do not play an important role when firm trailing stock returns are included among the explanatory variables, and (2) the relative importance of industry and macroeconomic variables is not conclusive. Are these results due to the use of different modeling techniques here? To address this concern, we also run OLS with the same model specifications as in table 4. We find variable significance very similar to those reported here, despite slightly worse model fit from OLS when continuous explanatory variables are included in the model. Even under OLS, firm trailing stock returns outweigh industry conditions in determining recovery, and industry variables do not dominate macroeconomic variables in driving recovery.

Therefore, the different results between this study and Acharya, Bharath, and Srinivasan (2007) are due to sample difference instead of methodology difference. We argue that results here should be more reliable, as our data are much more comprehensive and up to date.

Results From Alternative Seniority Indices

Further, we conduct analysis using different seniority variables. We replace seniority index with seniority index 3 and find very similar results: Seniority index 3 outweighs all other variables in explaining the default recovery. Results using seniority index 2 show that its role is weaker than either seniority index or seniority index 3, although it is still more important than macro-, industry- and firm-level variables, or other instrument-level variables.

Results From the Subsample of Revolvers and Term Loans and the Subsample of Bonds

We also conduct the same analysis on the subsample of only revolvers and term loans and on the subsample of only bonds to check if our conclusion on the seniority index may be driven by the large difference in this variable across bank loans and public bonds. The former subsample is more important to banks and the latter is more important to bond investors. Our main conclusions hold in both subsamples.

VI. Conclusion

In this study we examine the determinants of the outcomes of the default recovery process. A good understanding of what drives default recovery is important for all players in the financial markets, including investors, banks, rating agencies, and regulators, as well as academics. To more properly measure the relative seniority of an instrument in the debt structure of each defaulted firm, we propose a new instrument-level variable, called seniority index, that captures both the percentage of debt above and the percentage of debt pari passu. We find that seniority index is the most important determinant of recovery rates, explaining more recovery rate variations than the combination of all the commonly used instrument-level variables that are investigated in this study, including seniority class, collateral type, and percentage above. We therefore conclude that, when modeling recovery risk, it is critical to properly measure the relative position of a debt instrument in the debt structure of the firm following the absolute priority rule and to factor in both debt above and, more importantly, debt pari passu to the instrument under consideration.

Further, firm conditions, measured by the firm's trailing stock return, is the second most important determinant of recovery rates. For private firms, where market information is not available, industry and macro conditions can help. Unlike earlier studies, however, we do not find a dominant role for industry conditions and their relative contribution varies with the sample, model specification, and, most importantly, the choice of modeling technique.

References

Acharya, Viral.V., Sreedhar T. Bharath, and Anand Srinivasan. "Does Industry-Wide Distress Affect Defaulted Loans? Evidence from Creditor Recoveries." *Journal of Financial Economics* 85 (2007): 787–821.

Altman, Edward I. and Vellore Kishore. "Almost Everything You Wanted to Know About Recoveries on Defaulted Bonds." *Financial Analyst Journal* November/December (1996): 57-64.

Altman, Edward I., Andrea Resti, and Andrea Sironi. *Analyzing and Explaining Default Recovery Rates.* ISDA Research Report, London December (2001).

Altman, Edward I., Brooks Brady, Andrea Resti, and Andrea Sironi. "The Link Between Default and Recovery Rates: Theory, Empirical Evidence and Implications." *Journal of Business* 78 (2005): 2203–27.

Altman, Edward I., Andrea Resti, and Andrea Sironi. "Default Recovery Rates in Credit Risk Modeling: A Review of the Literature and Recent Evidence." *Journal of Finance Literature* Winter (2005): 21-45.

Breiman, Leo, Jerome H. Friedman, Richard A. Olshen, and C. J. Stone. *Classification and Regression Trees.* Belmont, CA: Wadworth International Group, 1984.

Bris, Arturo., S. Abraham Ravid, and Ronald Sverdlove. "Conflicts in Bankruptcy and the Sequence of Debt Issues." Working Paper, Rutgers University (2009).

Colla, Paolo, Filippo Ippolito, and Kai Li. "Debt Specialization." Working Paper, available at SSRN: http://ssrn.com/abstract=1520902, 2011.

Cremers, Martijn, Joost Driessen, and Pascal Maenhout. "Explaining the Level of Credit Spreads: Option-Implied Jump Risk Premia in a Firm Value Model." *Review of Financial Studies* 21 (2008): 2209–42.

De Servigny, Arnaud and Olivie Renault. *Measuring and Managing Credit Risk.* New York: The McGraw-Hill Companies, 2004.

Duffie, Darrell Andreas Eckner, Guillaume Horel, and Leandro Saita. "Frailty Correlated Default." *Journal of Finance* 64(5) (2009): 2089–123.

Elton, Edwin J., Martin J. Gruber, Deepak Agrawal, and Christopher Mann. "Explaining the Rate Spread on Corporate Bonds." *Journal of Finance* 56 (2001): 247–77.

Eom, Young Ho, Jean Helwege, and Jingzhi Huang. "Structural Models of Corporate Bond Pricing: An Empirical Analysis." *Review of Financial Studies* 17 (2004): 499-544.

Frye, Jon. "Collateral Damage." *Risk,* April (2000a): 91–4.

Frye, Jon. "Collateral Damage Detected." Working Paper, Federal Reserve Bank of Chicago, Emerging Issues Series 1-14, October 2000b.

Frye, Jon. "Depressing Recoveries." *Risk,* November (2000c): 108-11.

Gupton, Greg M., Christopher C. Finger, and Mickey Bhatia. *CreditMetrics Technical Document*, New York: J.P. Morgan & Co, 1997.

Gupton, Greg M., Daniel Gates, and Lea V. Carty. "Bank Loan Loss Given Default." *Moody's Special Comment* (November 2000).

Huang, Jingzhi and Ming Huang. "How Much of the Corporate-Treasury Yield Spread is Due to Credit Risk? " Working paper, Penn State University, 2002.

Longstaff, Francis A., Sanjay Mithal, and Eric Neis. "Corporate Yield Spreads: Default Risk or Liquidity? New Evidence from the Credit Default Swap Market." *The Journal of Finance* 60: (2005): 2213–2253.

Merton, Robert C. "On the Pricing of Corporate Debt: The Risk Structure of Interest Rates." *Journal of Finance* 29 (1974): 449–470.

Papke, Leslie E. and Jeffery. M. Wooldridge. "Econometric Methods for Fractional Response Variables with an Application to 401(k) Plan Participation Rates." *Journal of Applied Econometrics* 11 (1996): 619–32.

Pykhtin, Michael V. "Unexpected Recovery Risk." *Risk* August (2003): 74–8.

Qi, Min, Xiaofei Zhang, and Xinlei Zhao. "Unobservable Systematic Risk Factor and Default Prediction." Working paper, Office of the Comptroller of the Currency (2009).

Qi, Min and Xinlei Zhao. "Comparison of Modeling Methods for Loss Given Default." *Journal of Banking and Finance* 35 (2011): 2842-2855.

Rauh, Joshua and Amir Sufi. "Capital Structure and Debt Structure." *The Review of Financial Studies* 23 (2010): 4242-45.

Tang, Dragon and Hong Yan. "Market Conditions, Default Risk and Credit Spreads." *Journal of Banking and Finance* 34 (2010): 743–753

Varma, Praveen and Richard Cantor. "Determinants of Recovery Rates on Defaulted Bonds and Loans for North American Corporate Issuers: 1983–2003" *Journal of Fixed Income* 14 (2005): 29-44.

Table 1. Sample Distribution

Our sample is from Moody's Ultimate Recovery Database (URD). See footnote 14 in section III for grouping of collateral types.

Panel A: By Year

Year	# of obs.	Mean recovery rate	Year	# of obs.	Mean recovery rate
1987	24	83.64%	1998	45	39.29%
1988	7	44.75%	1999	75	58.24%
1989	31	36.62%	2000	110	42.49%
1990	33	44.33%	2001	230	45.52%
1991	82	74.63%	2002	314	42.12%
1992	24	93.53%	2003	132	75.24%
1993	21	51.56%	2004	59	73.54%
1994	14	70.09%	2005	97	81.81%
1995	26	54.08%	2006	16	57.24%
1996	4	52.32%	2007	11	79.61%
1997	14	60.04%	2008	57	73.99%
			2009	23	47.91%
Overall	1,449	56.33%			

Panel B: By Instrument and Collateral Type

Instrument type	# of obs.	Mean recovery rate	Collateral type	# of obs.	Mean recovery rate
Revolvers	254	82.45%	Capital stock	54	61.74%
Term loans	209	70.49%	Equipment	97	35.06%
Senior secured bonds	218	58.90%	Guarantees	4	97.65%
Senior unsecured bonds	483	52.69%	Inter-company debt	1	12.65%
Senior subordinated bonds	148	28.76%	Inventory, receivables, cash	52	93.48%
Subordinated bonds	120	25.79%	Most assets	395	77.37%
Junior bonds	17	18.36%	Other assets	23	79.36%
			Unsecured	791	44.15%
			Second lien	28	74.70%
			Third lien	4	56.64%

Table 2. Summary Statistics

Distance-to-default is a measure of volatility-adjusted leverage backed out of the Merton (1974) model. We use the Fama-French 12-industry definition. ROA is defined as the ratio of income before extraordinary items (Compustat data item 18) to assets (data item 6). Leverage is defined as the ratio of long-term debt (Compustat data item 9) plus debt in current liabilities (Compustat data item 34) to assets (Compustat data item 6). Tangibility is defined as the ratio of property, plant, and equipment (Compustat data item 8) to assets (Compustat data item 6). The market return is based on the NYSE-NASDAQ-AMEX value-weighted index. Percentage above measures the percentage of debt that is more senior than the instrument. Seniority index is equal to 1 minus percentage above minus ½ percentage pari passu. Seniority index 2 is 1 minus percentage above minus ⅓ percentage pari passu, and seniority index 3 is 1 minus percentage above minus ⅔ percentage pari passu.

Panel A: Summary Statistics

	Mean	Median
Aggregate distance-to-default	16.75	15.67
Trailing 12-month aggregate default rate	1.97%	1.98%
Trailing 12-month market return	0.03%	-3.92%
3-month T-bill rate	3.28%	3.36%
Industry distance-to-default	14.81	12.77
Industry ROA	−9.00%	−4.44%
Trailing 12-month industry default rate	3.44%	2.49%
Industry tangibility	0.34	0.32
Industry leverage	0.40	0.28
Industry stock returns	1.03%	−0.83%
Firm distance-to-default	11.94	4.64
Firm ROA	−12.81%	−8.91%
Firm tangibility	0.44	0.43
Firm leverage	0.60	0.57
Firm trailing 12-month stock returns	−65.26%	−84.77%
Percentage above	21.45%	9.07%
Seniority index	50.58%	50.00%
Seniority index 2	59.90%	66.67%
Seniority index 3	41.26%	33.33%

Panel B: Correlations

	Recovery rate	Percentage above	Seniority index	Seniority index 2
Percentage above	−0.4539			
Seniority index	0.5569	−0.8401		
Seniority index 2	0.5397	−0.9338	0.9786	
Seniority index 3	0.5507	−0.7136	0.9795	0.9170

Table 3. Results From the Regression Tree

This table presents results from the regression tree method (Breiman, Friedman, Olshen, and Stone, 1984). We include in the regression tree all instrument-level variables indicating instrument type and collateral type, as well as seniority index and percentage above. We have five firm-level variables (ROA, leverage, tangibility, distance-to-default, and trailing 12-month stock return), six industry-level variables (industry distance-to-default, trailing 12-month industry default rate, industry tangibility, industry leverage, trailing 12-month industry stock return, and industry ROA), four macro-level variables (trailing 12-month aggregate default rate, trailing 12-month stock market return, aggregate distance-to-default, and the three-month T-bill rate), and a utility industry dummy. In panel A, we require a minimum of 100 observations in each leaf, and we report results from each step. In panel B, we report variable contributions using different minimum size requirement at each leaf.

	Panel A: A Minimum of 100 Observations in Each Leaf With All Variables						
Step	Splitting variable	Value	R-squared		SSE		Cumulative variance explained
			In-sample	5-fold cross-validation	In-sample	5-fold cross-validation	
1	Seniority index	70.58%	0.231	0.230	166.44	166.72	50.10
2	Firm trailing 12-month stock return	−72.64%	0.385	0.383	133.27	133.66	83.26
3	Percentage above	0.10%	0.437	0.434	122.01	122.61	94.53
4	Percentage above	40.40%	0.482	0.478	112.21	112.95	104.33
5	Aggregate distance-to-default	14.44	0.496	0.492	109.14	109.95	107.40
6	Seniority index	26.98%	0.510	0.502	106.16	107.88	110.38
7	Industry leverage	0.43	0.528	0.519	102.27	104.17	114.27
8	Firm tangibility	59.82%	0.539	0.529	99.80	101.96	116.74
9	Firm trailing 12-month stock return	−85.71%	0.540	0.530	99.62	101.80	116.93

Table 3. (continued)

Panel B: Variable Contribution (Measured by SS) and Model Fit With Different Minimum Leaf Size Requirements

	Minimum leaf size requirement			
	80	60	40	20
Utility dummy	0	0	0	0
Junior bond	0	0	0	0
Revolver	0	0	0	0
Senior secured bond	0	0	0	0
Senior subordinated bond	0	0	0	0
Senior unsecured bond	0	0	0	0.24
Subordinated bond	0	0	0	0
Term loan	0	0	0	0
Seniority index	53.07	53.08	51.52	53.05
Capital stock	0	0	0	0
Equipment	0	0	0	0
Guarantee	0	0	0	0
Intellectual	0	0	0	0
Inter-company debt	0	0	0	0
Inventory, receivables and cash	0	0	0	0
Most assets	0	0	0	0
Other assets	0	0	0	0
Unsecured	0	0	0	1.74
Second lien	0	0	0	0
Third lien	0	0	0	0
Percentage above	21.06	21.06	22.04	22.55
Industry trailing 12-month default rate	0	0	0	2.49
Industry distance-to-default	0	0	2.43	3.44
Trailing 12-month aggregate stock market return	0	0	2.42	0
Trailing 12-month aggregate default rate	0.77	0.98	0	0.23
Aggregate distance-to-default	4.56	4.56	4.56	4.56
Industry stock market return	4.71	0	0	0
Industry return on assets (ROA)	0	0	0	1.98
Industry leverage	3.89	3.89	2.34	3.86
Industry tangibility	0	0	5.18	10.86
Firm distance-to-default	5.06	11.03	15.24	11.15
Firm leverage	0	0.77	0.37	4.04
Firm return on assets (ROA)	0	0	0	1.91
Firm tangibility	0.94	5.78	8.49	9.80
Firm trailing 12-month stock return	33.38	33.17	33.17	33.91
Three-month T-bill rate	0	1.69	0.62	2.77
Total SS explained	127.43	136.01	148.38	168.58
R-squared				
In-sample	0.59	0.63	0.69	0.78
5-fold cross-validation	0.58	0.62	0.67	0.76

Table 4. Results From the Fractional Response Regression

This table report results from the fractional response regression. The base case for instrument types is subordinated bond, and the base case for collateral types is most assets. Default rate, stock return, and three-month T-bill are reported in percentages.

Panel A: Instrument and Collateral Type						
	Model 1		Model 2		Model 3	
	Coeff.	P-value	Coeff.	P-value	Coeff.	P-value
Seniority index						
Revolvers	2.624	0.001			2.048	0.001
Term loans	1.940	0.001			1.426	0.001
Senior secured bonds	1.247	0.001			1.604	0.001
Senior unsecured bonds	1.086	0.001			1.089	0.001
Senior subordinated bonds	0.172	0.001			0.168	0.001
Junior bonds	−0.723	0.002			−0.653	0.004
Capital stock			−0.638	0.001	−0.637	0.001
Equipment			−1.733	0.001	−1.665	0.001
Guarantees			2.612	0.633	2.440	0.660
Inter-company debt			−3.049	0.501	−2.961	0.509
Inventory, receivables, and cash			1.521	0.001	1.281	0.001
Other assets			0.230	0.100	0.189	0.184
Unsecured			−1.449	0.001	−0.546	0.001
Second lien			−0.202	0.052	−0.074	0.496
Third lien			−1.074	0.045	−0.224	0.720
Utility dummy	1.146	0.001	0.971	0.001	0.878	0.001
Intercept	−1.114	0.001	1.116	0.001	−0.553	0.001
SSE	160.27		166.71		152.40	
Adj. R-squared	0.256		0.225		0.288	

Panel B: Seniority Index, Percentage Above, Instrument, and Collateral Type

	Model 4		Model 5		Model 6		Model 7		Model 8		Model 9	
	Coeff.	P-value	Coeff.	P-value	Coeff.	P-value	Coeff.	P-value	Coeff.	P-value	Coeff.	P-value
Percent above			-2.752	0.001	0.859	0.001			-1.679	0.001	1.085	0.001
Seniority index	4.291	0.001			5.202	0.001	3.812	0.001				
Revolvers							0.896	0.001	1.333	0.001	1.031	0.001
Term loans							0.370	0.003	0.761	0.003	5.029	0.494
Senior secured bonds							1.054	0.001	1.069	0.001	1.248	0.001
Senior unsecured bonds							0.478	0.001	0.620	0.001	0.572	0.001
Senior subordinated bonds							0.036	0.379	0.116	0.004	0.014	0.732
Junior bonds							0.086	0.708	-0.069	0.767	-0.097	0.676
Capital stock							-0.358	0.001	-0.459	0.001	-0.389	0.001
Equipment							-1.285	0.001	-1.672	0.001	-1.163	0.001
Guarantees							3.193	0.598	2.507	0.674	2.966	0.674
Inter-company debt							-3.189	0.435	-2.828	0.517	-3.006	0.517
Inventory, receivables, and cash							1.369	0.001	1.295	0.001	1.400	0.001
Other assets							0.001	0.995	0.145	0.312	-0.008	0.954
Unsecured							0.207	0.003	-0.370	0.001	0.371	0.001
Second lien							0.372	0.004	0.364	0.002	0.269	0.047
Third lien							0.368	0.563	-0.123	0.842	0.733	0.277
Utility dummy	1.031	0.001	0.967	0.001	1.046	0.001	0.841	0.001	0.831	0.001	0.857	0.001
Intercept	-1.947	0.001	0.757	0.001	-2.567	0.001	-2.262	0.001	0.154	0.102	-3.281	0.102
SSE	145.35		167.32		144.905		135.95		144.89		135.34	
Adj. R-squared	0.328		0.226		0.3294		0.365		0.323		0.367	

Panel C: Instrument and Firm-Level Variables

	Model 7 Coeff.	Model 7 P-value	Model 10 Coeff.	Model 10 P-value	Model 11 Coeff.	Model 11 P-value	Model 12 Coeff.	Model 12 P-value	Model 13 Coeff.	Model 13 P-value	Model 14 Coeff.	Model 14 P-value
Seniority index	3.812	0.001	3.784	0.001	3.935	0.001	3.704	0.001	4.003	0.001	4.042	0.001
Firm distance-to-default			0.274	0.001							−0.368	0.001
Firm ROA					1.424	0.001					1.264	0.001
Firm tangibility							1.819	0.001			1.945	0.001
Firm trailing 12-month stock returns									1.706	0.001	1.577	0.001
Intercept	−2.262	0.001	−2.244	0.001	−2.105	0.001	−2.813	0.001	−1.361	0.001	−2.052	0.001
Instrument types	Yes		Yes		Yes		Yes			Yes		
Collateral types	Yes		Yes		Yes		Yes			Yes		
Utility dummy	Yes		Yes		Yes		Yes	Yes		Yes		
SSE	135.95		135.11		130.58		129.14	Yes	115.71	Yes	106.87	
Adj. R-squared	0.365		0.368		0.389		0.396	Yes	0.459	Yes	0.499	

Panel D: Instrument, Firm, Industry, and Economy Level Variables

	Model 15		Model 16		Model 17		Model 18		Model 19		Model 20	
	Coeff.	P-value	Coeff.	P-value	Coeff.	P-value	Coeff.	P-value	Coeff.	P-value	Coeff.	P-value
Seniority index	3.942	0.001	3.873	0.001	4.389	0.001	4.439	0.001	4.017	0.001	4.326	0.001
Firm ROA	1.185	0.001	0.708	0.001	1.054	0.001	0.901	0.001				
Firm tangibility	1.945	0.001	1.931	0.001	1.942	0.001	1.772	0.001				
Firm trailing 12-month stock returns	1.489	0.001	1.094	0.001	1.417	0.001	1.089	0.001				
Industry distance-to-default			11.069	0.001			8.883	0.001	11.484	0.001		
Industry stock market returns			-0.052	0.001			-0.074	0.001	-0.044	0.001		
Industry tangibility			0.770	0.001				0.037	2.124	0.001		
Trailing 12-month aggregate default rate					-5.225	0.001 0.465	-2.975	0.001			-5.246	0.001
3-month T-bill rate					-2.177	0.001	-2.363	0.001			-2.678	0.001
Stock market returns					0.041	0.001	0.080	0.001			0.095	0.001
Intercept	-1.948	0.001	-3.491	0.001	-0.168	0.311	-2.003	0.001	-4.554	0.001	-0.353	0.011
Instrument types	Yes		Yes		Yes		Yes		Yes		Yes	
Collateral types	Yes		Yes		Yes		Yes		Yes		Yes	
Utility dummy	Yes		Yes		Yes		Yes		Yes		Yes	
SSE	107.12		95.53		94.36		88.82		116.71		117.86	
Adj. R-squared	0.498		0.552		0.557		0.582		0.454		0.448	

35

Figure 1. Results From Regression Tree Model 1

This figure presents results from the regression tree method (Breiman, Friedman, Olshen, and Stone, 1984). We include in the regression tree all instrument-level variables indicating instrument type and collateral type, as well as seniority index and percentage above. We have five firm-level variables (ROA, leverage, tangibility, distance-to-default, and trailing 12-month stock return), six industry-level variables (industry distance-to-default, trailing 12-month industry default rate, industry tangibility, industry leverage, trailing 12-month industry stock return, and industry ROA), four macro-level variables (trailing 12-month aggregate default rate, trailing 12-month stock market return, aggregate distance-to-default, and the three-month T-bill rate), and a utility industry dummy. We require a minimum of 100 observations in each leaf. Model fit from each step is reported in panel A of table 3.

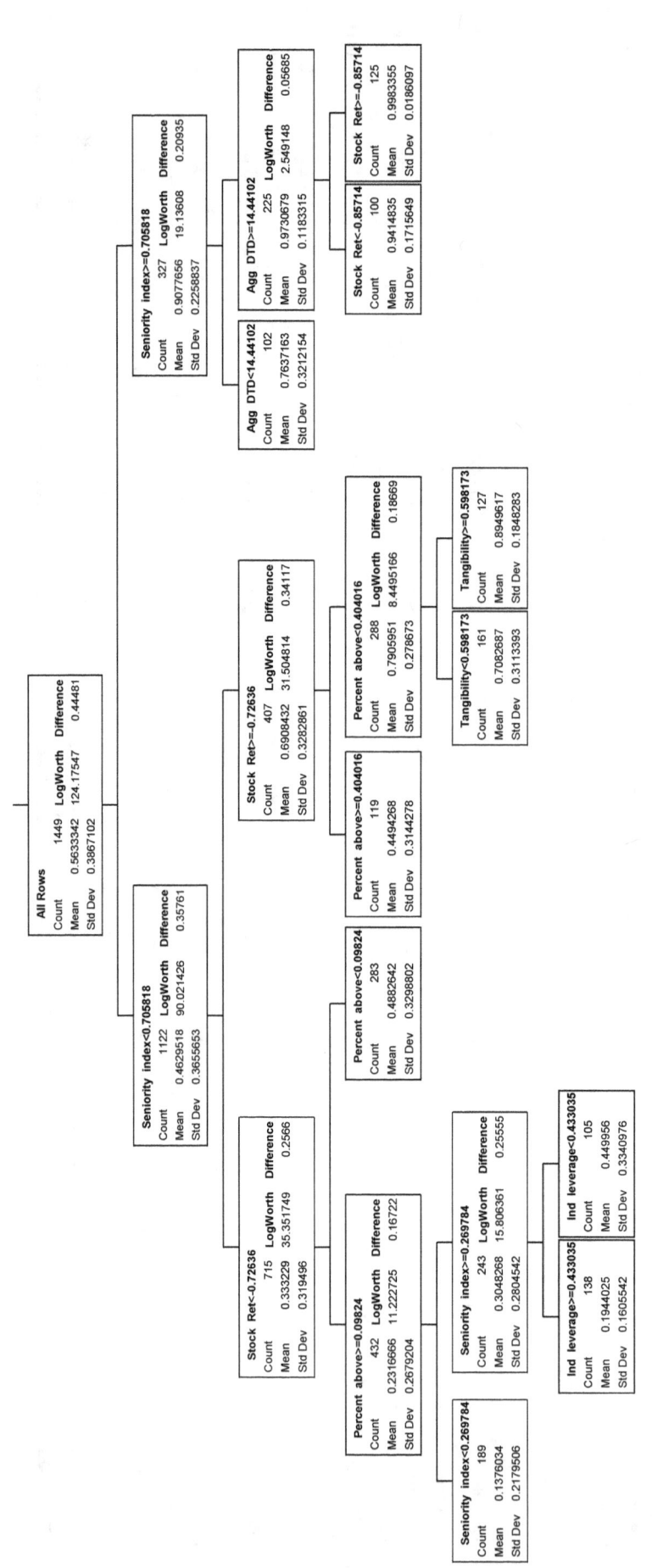

36

Figure 2. Contribution from Each Variable in Regression Tree Model 1

This figure presents results on variable contribution from the regression tree in figure 1.

Column Contributions

Term	Number of Splits	SS	
Utility_dummy	0	0	
Junior	0	0	
Revolver	0	0	
Senior_secure	0	0	
Senior_subordinated	0	0	
Senior_unsecure	0	0	
Subordinated	0	0	
Term_loan	0	0	
Seniority_index	2	53.0718534	
Capital_stock	0	0	
Equipment	0	0	
Guarantees	0	0	
Inter_company_debt	0	0	
Inven_AR_cash	0	0	
Most_assets	0	0	
Other_assets	0	0	
Unsecured	0	0	
Second_lien	0	0	
Third_lien	0	0	
Percent_above	2	21.0594834	
Ind_Dft_Rate	0	0	
Ind_DTD	0	0	
Mkt_Ret	0	0	
Agg_Dft_Rate	0	0	
Agg_DTD	1	3.07600896	
Ind_Ret	0	0	
Ind_ROA	0	0	
Ind_leverage	1	3.89426695	
Ind_tangibility	0	0	
DTD	0	0	
Leverage	0	0	
ROA	0	0	
Tangibility	1	2.47453266	
Stock_Ret	2	33.3489256	
TBill_rate	0	0	
Total	9	116.925071	

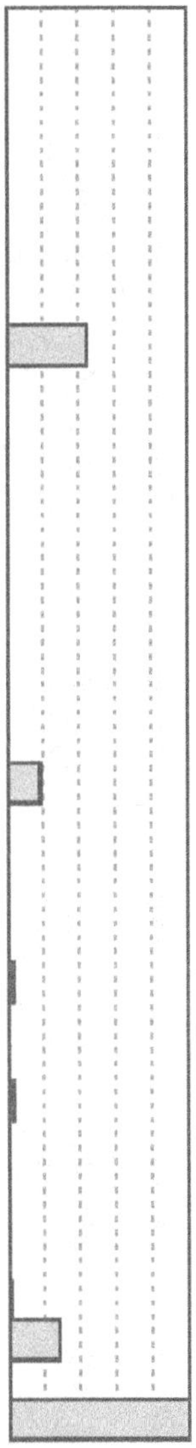

Figure 3. Model Fit and Contributions From Each Variable: Regression Tree Model 2—Excluding Percentage Above

The difference between this regression tree and the tree in figure 1 is that we lock out percentage above from this tree. The tree itself is not reported to save space.

Column Contributions

Term	Number of Splits	SS
Utility_dummy	0	0
Junior	0	0
Revolver	0	0
Senior_secure	0	0
Senior_subordinated	0	0
Senior_unsecure	0	0
Subordinated	0	0
Term_loan	0	0
Seniority_index	3	66.7049867
Capital_stock	0	0
Equipment	0	0
Guarantees	0	0
Intellectual	0	0
Inter_company_debt	0	0
Inven_AR_cash	0	0
Most_assets	0	0
Other_assets	0	0
Unsecured	0	0
Second_lien	0	0
Third_lien	0	0
Percent_above	0	0
Ind_Dft_Rate	0	0
Ind_DTD	0	0
Mkt_Ret	0	0
Agg_Dft_Rate	1	4.9725328
Agg_DTD	1	3.07600896
Ind_Ret	0	0
Ind_ROA	0	0
Ind_leverage	0	0
Ind_tangibility	0	0
DTD	1	10.5402678
Leverage	0	0
ROA	0	0
Tangibility	1	2.11769702
Stock_Ret	3	33.3726981
TBill_rate	1	2.22334299
Total	11	123.007534

	SSE	RSquare
5-fold cross-validation	95.353342	0.5597
Overall	93.5332663	0.5681

Figure 4. Model Fit and Contributions From Each Variable: Regression Tree Model 3—Excluding Seniority Index

The difference between this regression tree and the tree in figure 1 is that we lock out seniority index from this tree. The tree itself is not reported to save space.

Column Contributions

Term	Number of Splits	SS
Utility_dummy	0	0
Junior	0	0
Revolver	0	0
Senior_secure	0	0
Senior_subordinated	0	0
Senior_unsecure	0	0
Subordinated	0	0
Term_loan	0	0
Seniority_index	0	0
Capital_stock	0	0
Equipment	0	0
Guarantees	0	0
Intellectual	0	0
Inter_company_debt	0	0
Inven_AR_cash	0	0
Most_assets	0	0
Other_assets	0	0
Unsecured	0	0
Second_lien	0	0
Third_lien	0	0
Percent_above	2	45.05978
Ind_Dft_Rate	0	0
Ind_DTD	0	0
Mkt_Ret	0	0
Agg_Dft_Rate	1	0.3415914
Agg_DTD	1	16.08387
Ind_Ret	0	0
Ind_ROA	0	0
Ind_leverage	2	4.12350333
Ind_tang bility	0	0
DTD	1	9.42416214
Leverage	0	0
ROA	1	7.28866601
Tangibility	1	5.36423685
Stock_Ret	1	25.6571745
TBill_rate	0	0
Total	10	113.342985

	SSE	RSquare
5-fold cross-validation	104.871989	0.5157
Overall	103.197816	0.5234

Figure 5. Model Fit and Contributions From Each Variable: Regression Tree Model 4—Excluding Both Seniority Index and Percentage Above

The difference between this regression tree and the tree in figure 1 is that we lock out both seniority index and percentage above from this tree. The tree itself is not reported to save space.

Column Contributions

Term	Number of Splits	SS	
Utility_dummy	0	0	
Junior	0	0	
Revolver	1	21.7135461	
Senior_secure	0	0	
Senior_subordinated	0	0	
Senior_unsecure	0	0	
Subordinated	0	0	
Term_loan	0	0	
Seniority_index	0	0	
Capital_stock	0	0	
Equipment	0	0	
Guarantees	0	0	
Intellectual	0	0	
Inter_company_debt	0	0	
Inven_AR_cash	0	0	
Most_assets	1	15.514321	
Other_assets	0	0	
Unsecured	2	11.1506826	
Second_lien	0	0	
Third_lien	0	0	
Percent_above	0	0	
Ind_Dft_Rate	1	2.0459989	
Ind_DTD	0	0	
Mkt_Ret	0	0	
Agg_Dft_Rate	0	0	
Agg_DTD	1	1.21489251	
Ind_Ret	1	0.74330799	
Ind_ROA	0	0	
Ind_leverage	0	0	
Ind_tangibility	0	0	
DTD	2	15.3498941	
Leverage	0	0	
ROA	0	0	
Tangibility	0	0	
Stock_Ret	1	31.1341986	
TBill_rate	0	0	
Total	10	98.8668418	

	SSE	RSquare
5-fold cross-validation	120.522388	0.4434
Overall	117.673959	0.4566

Figure 6. Model Fit and Contributions From Each Variable: Regression Tree Model 5—Excluding Firm Stock Returns, Seniority Index, and Percentage Above

The difference between this regression tree and the tree in figure 1 is that we lock out seniority index, percentage above and firm stock return from this tree. The tree itself is not reported to save space.

Column Contributions

Term	Number of Splits	SS	
Utility_dummy	0	0	
Junior	0	0	
Revolver	1	23.9772857	
Senior_secure	0	0	
Senior_subordinated	0	0	
Senior_unsecure	0	0	
Subordinated	0	0	
Term_loan	1	12.5079398	
Seniority_index	0	0	
Capital_stock	0	0	
Equipment	0	0	
Guarantees	0	0	
Intellectual	0	0	
Inter_company_debt	0	0	
Inven_AR_cash	0	0	
Most_assets	0	0	
Other_assets	0	0	
Unsecured	2	4.60554152	
Second_lien	0	0	
Third_lien	0	0	
Percent_above	0	0	
Ind_Dft_Rate	0	0	
Ind_DTD	1	22.3239209	
Mkt_Ret	1	1.49624684	
Agg_Dft_Rate	0	0	
Agg_DTD	0	0	
Ind_Ret	0	0	
Ind_ROA	0	0	
Ind_leverage	0	0	
Ind_tang bility	0	0	
DTD	0	0	
Leverage	0	0	
ROA	1	3.05512056	
Tangibility	1	7.43877757	
Stock_Ret	0	0	
TBill_rate	1	9.28029206	
Total	9	84.6851249	

	SSE	RSquare
5-fold cross-validation	134.670135	0.3781
Overall	131.855676	0.3911